HOW FAST THE RIVER ROSE

New Poems (2019-2023)

The Porcupine Press
115 Chemin du Clos de Ségaras
30700 Montaren
France
porcupinepressfr@gmail.com

Design and Typesetting by David Maes

Published 2024 by The Porcupine Press
Printed in the United States of America

ISBN : 978-0-9908597-8-9

HOW FAST THE RIVER ROSE

New Poems (2019-2023)

by

Harvey Mudd

THE PORCUPINE PRESS

I

TITLES OF POEMS

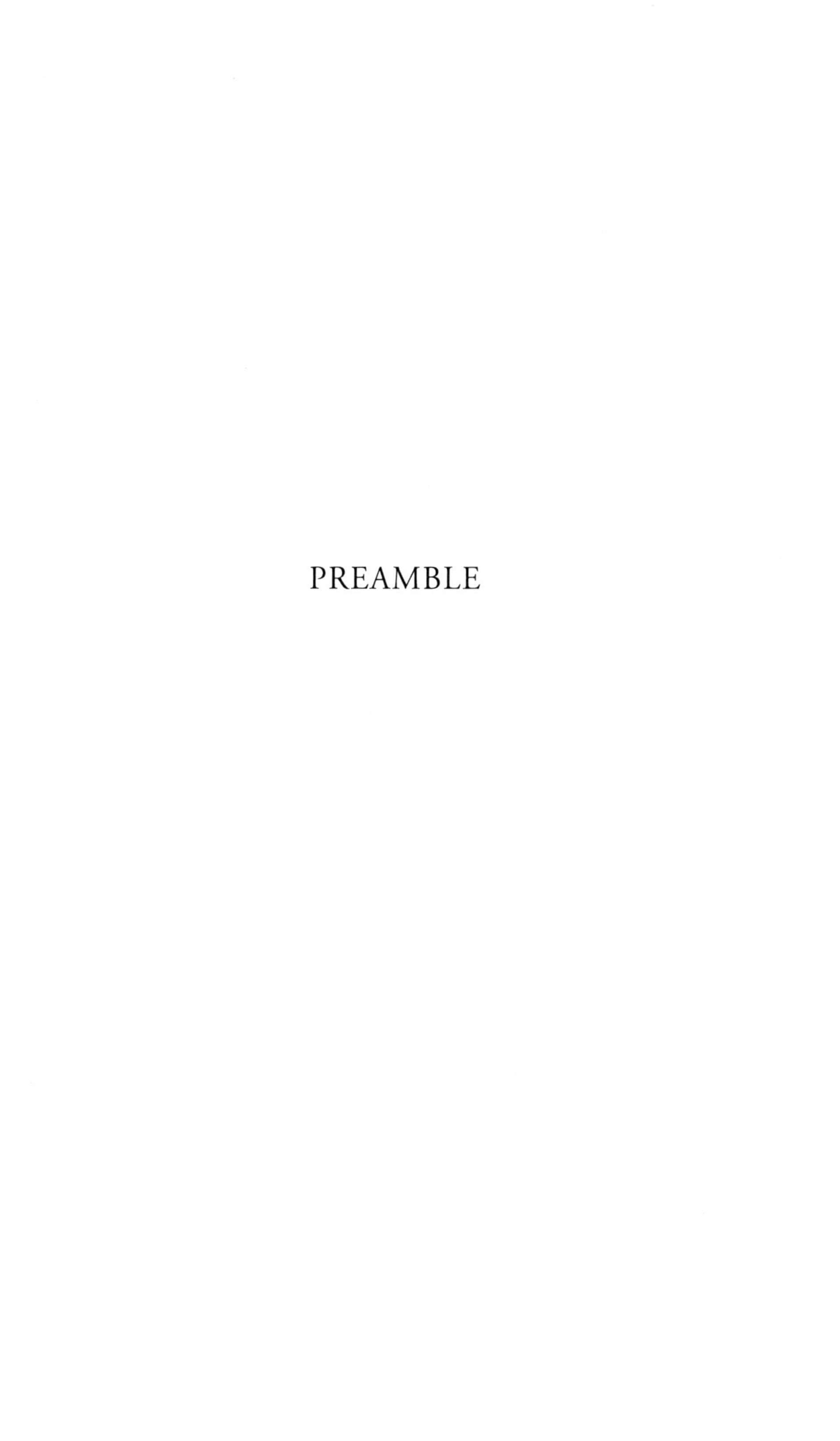

PREAMBLE

The Distant Rooster

I listen to the morning birds
in the flowering hawthorn
and to the distant rooster
two farms down.
Not musical, my rooster friend,
but a master of boasts and jibes,
just the annoying sort of thing
to get me out of bed.

I get the chickens off their perches,
the rooster says,
chickens, dumb or pretty,
the work's the same,
get them to the gravel, straw, and dust,
where they do what chickens must.
And get the ducks, with their flat
and orange feet, down to the pond
where they swim about
and quack their single syllable of praise to god,
either the one who drops hailstones
on their heads,
or the one that keeps a chopping block
behind the shed.

So get your poems awake,
the insistent rooster crows,
and at their jobs,
make them sing while the sun rises,
yes, you sing too, though you may spook the sheep
or insult the king, sing,
sing while still you can.
It means you are alive and free.

Sing your heart out,
just as I, each morning, do.

II

I

I took a Detour

I set out for home, our house
among the sunflower fields,
to the kitchen with its pans and pantry shelves,
the piles of bedside books,
and geraniums in clay pots
on the windowsill.
I looked forward to being sure
of what comes next,
that we'd eat our meal, talk a while,
laugh, describe the magpies in the fields,
how strong the wind had been,
then sleep side by side,
and know that in the morning
we'd resume.

But on this afternoon,
I took an unfamiliar route.
I'd go around
what I already knew.

It was late and time seemed tilted.
The sunlight, slanting through
a flickering mesh of speed,
threw long shadows
along the rows of olive trees.

Clouds rose up behind Ventoux.
In the light of the setting sun,
the piles of cumulous
made the mountain seem smaller.

The clouds, still white,
shone like marble,
like temples and senates,
like towers and palaces.
An enchanted civilization,
one built of vapor.

As the sun went lower,
the clouds turned orange
and seemed ablaze.
What I'd just seen in splendor
was being consumed by fire.

I stopped the car to watch.
The spectacle was soon over.
I sat behind the steering wheel,
gripping it, as if frightened
or overwhelmed by sorrow.

I thought of home.
The road ahead was narrow
and night was gathering.
I considered turning back,
returning along the way I'd come,
but I'd come too far along,
so went on.

Lament of the Frontier Guard

after Li Po (701-762),
via Ezra Pound (1885-1972)

We huddle by our fire
and tell stories about absent comrades,
and about the cities
that we had besieged and ruined.
In the summer it's the same,
but without the fire.

Fragments of the days
we no longer bother with
lie on the trail that we take
to our watch tower.
In the twilight they glint
like shards of glass.

For one hundred years
bullets have exhausted themselves
against the walls
of this nameless village,
this pathetic gathering of humans
trapped in history
with their animals.

We have been sent
to the edge of the world.
In ancient times
we were abandoned at our posts
and left to the tigers.
There are no more tigers,
just lice and the lies they tell us
about the empire
and the glories still to come.

We look at the moon with longing
and masturbate.
Our seed is sterile.
Our socks rot.

Venus and Mars

Venus, Lucretius says,
is behind the eternal dance, the lust
for life, and still more life,
still more and more.
New life is her one true love
and spring her season.
What goes on in bedrooms
is how she whiles away the months
until spring returns.

Occasionally she brings calm
to the killing fields,
arranges truces between men
who glut on glory and on slaughter.
Mars, most terrible, Great War himself,
sometimes succumbs to her.
Hands stained with blood and gore,
he lays his massive head
on her lap, looks up,
sees beauty, and adores.
She of Mars is not even fond,
not approving of what he does for work.
Destruction's easy, creation's harder.
But they share the world,
so she picks from his matted hair
bits of this and that.
"Come lie with me," she says,
"but clean up first."

III

IV

In these Fields of France

Not long past, but beyond
what I can remember,
armies gathered on these fields,
kingdoms clashed,
and men died in great number.
In my little town alone
eighty-six died before slaughter ended,
sons, husbands, fathers.
Their names are on a pedestal in the square,
but as the frenzy took hold,
no name, no person, mattered,
and we became like particles of ash
swirled up in the smoke of burning cities,
or like droplets of water absorbed
and disappearing
into the passing fogs of time.
And we, who thought ourselves
as having some small worth as men,
understood, as we fell,
something sad and terrible
about the fatal carelessness
of human kind.

There's no comedy here on earth,
just strife and suffering
as the wrathful,
the fevered, and the mad
devour their young
and then each other.

*

Here in France, where I live,
those who survived came home
and passed on the genes
for violence and folly,
for poetry and prayer.
And the gene that permits forgetting
and so today,
one hundred fifteen years after,
white clouds drift across a flawless sky,
and the fields are just as we remembered them,
green, unscarred, new.

*

Though occasionally these same fields
cough up a shell that had not exploded.
It's after the thaw usually,
when the earth relaxes.
Whose shell it was no longer matters,
only that it might still be live.
The fire brigade comes in a heavy truck,
bright red, that tears up the field.
And we, the innocents in the fairy tale
that we have told our selves since time began
are saved again, still believing
that God protects us
and that we will live forever.

And sometimes bones emerge.
The children found some in an eroded gully,
white sticks, curved and smooth,
so unlike branches that even the children knew.

They brought them to us.
There were more, they said,
just so big, and showed us
with their hands.
Bones too small for cow,
too big for rabbit,
possibly human then.
For this, we call our priest.

Father Jean is a young man,
younger than my son.
He remembers nothing
of nineteen sixteen,
or of forty four, nor could he,
not yet born.
Of the years of dread,
Russia and the bomb, the Cold War,
he has no memory either.
"But I've had anxieties," he says,
"Today, the entire Middle East.
And Ukraine, war again in Europe."
What does he understand? I wait.
"My grandfather," he says, " lived to ninety years
and he remembered nineteen seventeen,
almost died, he told me,
in these same fields, almost buried alive
in a trench that had collapsed
and filled with stinking mud."

We walk on.
We go to find the gulley
as the children had described it,
with perhaps more bones hidden

beneath the years and years
of rotting leaves.
We walk through the fields,
past grazing cows, animals
slow and calm, not even curious.
He carries a canvas bag,
a garden spade, his rosary,
and his book of prayers.
His cassock drags through tall grass
and stirs up clouds of pollen.
I sneeze. Easter soon,
the celebration of the only man who died
and came back alive.

*

It's grass, I think, that's the real miracle.
It healed these fields.
But somewhere else
the miracle comes undone.
The end of days?
Armageddon at last?
"How long we've waited,"
the most intense among us say.
"We despoiled the earth
because we found it worthless.
We acquired great riches,
but soon will ascend into heaven
and there receive our last and best reward.
We will leave the rest of you behind,
to burn, to drown,
as you deserve,
or to be blinded by the flash."

And if Messiah does come this second time,
as history comes around again, repeats itself, rephrases,
if He finds his way
through the rubble and the weeds,
He'll find us, Jean and I,
a man of God and a man without,
but friends,
sitting in the dismal boneyard
that the world's become
with the fragments of an unknown soldier
in a canvas bag.

A Very Short Explanation

Sunlight falls everywhere,
falls like ash from a catastrophe
so distant in the past
that it's been forgotten.

The sunlight is owned by no one
so poor men gather it.
They are gleaners.
Their thumbs and fingers
contract around the handles
of their shovels.
Their hands are deformed.
They can't play the piano
or write with a pencil.

The sunlight is heavy,
but the men do not complain.
They load it into wagons
and set out for the city
where they will sell it.
But when they arrive, night
has already has fallen.
They've come too late.

They dump the sunlight
by the roadside,
in the gutters, into rubbish tips,
into abandoned mine shafts
and the catacombs.

As they file out of the city,
the wheels of their empty wagons
rattle on the cobble stones,
a sound like that of dry bones
shaken in a burlap sack.

They don't look back.
They start over.
They remember nothing.
They are history,
yet they know nothing of it.

II

The Messenger

The horse at a distance
fit the idea of Horse perfectly.
I mistook it for an avatar of God.
It was large, white, and slow,
just as God must be.
To those of us who call the neighborhood
of the LaFarge concrete plant
our home, it seemed a marvel.

I approached the Horse.
It was grazing.
The clouds turned gray,
heavy, brooding, filled with water.
They gathered over the plant,
which has a silo, tall and white,
like a steeple. This is the cathedral
of *Saint Cement,*
the cult of the Job-Site-Ready.
Below the steeple
are bins and hoppers
containing sand and gravel,
the raw materials
of worlds yet unmade.

As the storm gathered,
Divinities clashed in the shaking air.
The horse was calm
but I was afraid.
In my youth I'd had notions

that were heretical,
that Jimi Hendrix
was the archangel,
Gabriel the messenger,
come back as Jimi,
his wand a Fender Stratocaster,
an instrument like a branch of lilies
with electric strings.

Then the Thunder spoke.
"I," the clouds roiled and flashed
and chimed like a Hendrix riff,
"I," the Voice again,
"do not walk about on four legs
or eat grass."

Was it God's own voice I heard?
I was not sure.
"I," the Voice went on,
strumming with all its fingers
on the trembling air,
"don't do concrete.
I don't care for roads or bridges,
or airports with cantilevered roofs
or any of your brainless *isms*."

The sky rippled with light.
The Voice spoke again.
"Here's the news. It's not good.
You who were once blessed
with bounties without number
have made a great mess of things.
Creation is becoming unbuilt
and the fault is yours."

The sky then fell upon us
like a sack of fury ripped open.
The end of the world commenced.
The rain hammered,
a din like the rolling of stones
in a flooding stream.
Like a fatwa.
Like ex-communication.

I took shelter and survived.
But it will happen again;
I'll be caught in the open
and be soaked to the skin.

But this time spared,
I turned toward home.
I took the long route.
It was more scenic.

The horse raised its head
and watched me go.

> Jimi, who is both dead
> and immortal,
> was caught up in clouds
> and ascended.
> "There must be some way out of here,"
> thought Jimi.

The Plague Year

Saint Roche believed that God
had sent the plague
to test mankind's love for Him.
Roche had the wound,
loved God, and passed the test.

Roche was a good man.
He held the hands of the dying,
and wiped their brows.

And he had a dog.

    The dog,
    if saintliness there ever was,
    was saintly.
    He soothed the fearful swelling
    on his master's leg
    with a gentle tongue.
    He brought a loaf of bread.
    He asked only for a word,
    a pat, a scratch
    behind the ears.

When his master died,
a cloud came down,
a flurry of angels' wings,
a rapturous ruckus,
and Roche ascended.

But dog was left behind.
No place in Paradise for dogs,
not on the right hand
or the left hand either,
not even in the yard.

Now he wanders through
the empty streets
of Brooklyn, the Bronx, and Queens.
He hears the sirens
and dodges ambulances.
When he comes to visit
I put out a bowl of kibble
and water from the tap.
Then he goes off.
He's on his own,
like the rest of us.

V

Explaining Death to Dogs

Three dogs, their muzzles
flecked with gray,
wait beneath a tree.
The dogs are old.
Of dying they know nothing.
They wait. They do not question.
Dogs don't.

If they must die,
they do. They will not run or hide.
They do not complain
unless there's pain,
a wound, a kick.
They need no explanation.
It's we who do.

Owls in the River Wood

My home is here
in the river wood.
I cut rushes with the sickle moon
and bind them with vines.
I am building a house
and preparing an altar.

Owls slide through the night
on silent wings.
Invisible, they perch
on the invisible rafters of my house.
They sit next to the invisible gods
that I invite to my altar.

The owls in the river wood
are harbingers of death.
I like the sound that they make,
the single note,
with nothing wanting,
nothing wasted, nothing before,
nothing after.

I Found my Bed Unmade

Along the darkened hall,
a light bulb out,
and past the extra room,
I came to the bedroom
that I've called my own
for as long as I remember.
I found my bed unmade.
There was the naked mattress,
depressed where we,
then I alone, had lain
and tossed and turned
for so many nights,
for years and years.

I had washed the sheets
and hung them out to dry
in the bright spring sun,
the smell of wet cotton
in the dry air of morning,
the wooden clothes pins,
worn and experienced,
like the fingers of a washer woman.
A light breeze stirred my hair.
I felt the warmth of sun on my back
as I stretched the sheets
along the line behind the olive trees.

I'd hung them out,
but then forgot.

I cooked my meal
and drank some wine.
The house seemed large,
strangely empty, and unfamiliar,
as if it were not my house
but a vessel traveling in space
with me inside it.
I was alone,
almost afraid.

I cleaned the dishes
thought of sleep.
I went down the hall.
The moon was up,
the garden washed in moonlight.
Through the window,
I saw the sheets,
suspended as I'd left them.
They were stirring slightly,
fluttering, like ghosts caught speaking.
Where has our sleeper gone?
they asked.

Prelude and Fugue

Our church sits on the headland,
overlooking the river and the bay;
and beyond, over the sandbars
that rise up as the tide goes out,
we see the wide Atlantic.
The continent is behind us,
just down the road, as I think of it,
and this New England corner
of that once unknown place
is Massachusetts.

Our church is called St. Elizabeth's,
so named by our ancestors
after the war between the states
as a gesture of faith about the future.
Elizabeth, the saint,
is protector of the homeless,
the poor, and perhaps,
they thought, of wounded soldiers.
Our ancestors were generous people.
Our memory of them is kept close by,
in the burial ground
behind the church, a traditional field,
white headstones
of Massachusetts marble
too soft to hold an inscription
much longer than three hundred years.
The church is of sandstone,

the same stone that built New York City
before the age of steel and glass.
It's a New England stone also,
from Connecticut, reddish brown,
a bit rough to the touch.
It doesn't polish.

Of the men who extracted,
cut, and shaped the stone,
then raised it, course by course,
no trace remains, no names,
not even payroll pages
marked with x for pay received.
No one remembers.
Our town history notes
only that they were Italians.

Saint Elizabeth had no room
for immigrants.
She did not despise them,
but didn't notice either.
They came, thus, unblessed and unprotected
into the promised land.
Some remained the poorest of the poor,
whose children died young
in the tenements.
Some became bakers,
some thieves, some went on
as they'd come, as stone cutters.
Their children became Americans.
The quarries where they cut the stone
are now formless pits
filled with water.

*

When we were children
we played in the church yard,
but not among the headstones
because we were afraid.
A little older, the dark oak pews,
the stone columns and arched ceilings
formed a sheltering,
a safe place for innocence and secrets.
I remember how we squeezed
into the confessional and stole
first kisses. I remember
the sweet smell of your hair.
Washed in rainwater, you told me.

*

In the mild summer of our sixteenth year,
we walked in the quiet glade
of Yankee graves.
"Lost at Sea," is a common legend,
for ours was a sailor's town,
the China trade,
or "American Expeditionary Force
1917, killed in action, Belleau Wood,"
or the man who wanted to be remembered
for what he did for work, "surveyor."
But most common is "beloved..." Here
your father rests,
your mother too, and all your clan.
The cemetery is like the scrapbook
of the town. It told its story.
We were young and in love,
and we believed our story would outlast them all.

I've not been back for fifty years.
You married and moved away.
I had thought you'd stay.

*

The church, washed by salt fogs,
its sandstone walls
scraped by wind, wears down.
For one hundred and twenty years
it has resisted, but someday
it will be abandoned,
a relic of a bygone age
when people believed in a loving god,
and America was united
by a noble purpose.

This Sunday, the congregation is smaller.
No one knew me.
I'd been away too long.
They sang their favorite hymns.
"Rock of Ages, cleft for me,
let me hid myself in thee."
I listened but did not sing.
I did not belong.

When all departed,
I stayed behind.
Below the bluff
I could hear the patient persuasion
of ocean, the unceasing dialogue
between waves and land.
The beach where we played as children
was being swept away.

And the bluff too, each year
a little more collapses,
and the continent diminishes.

III

VII

Van Gogh and the Crows

And the lord said
"let there be crows,"
and there were.
A great parliament of them
tumbled out
of the wintery clouds,

and this was not
on the first day of creation,
but well into the undoing
of it, as may be the case.

Fifty or sixty crows,
flapping and cawing and
bumping each into another.
They settled into the olive grove
by my neighbor's house.

Clouds gathered,
gray clouds. Snow maybe.

Vincent saw a flock of crows
in a wheat field.
He painted them flying off.
It was the last day of his life.
He painted the clouds
and a road.

VIII

The Temptation of Saint Anthony

after Hieronymus Bosch

A raven brought me bread,
then last week's *Le Monde*,
so torn and stained
that I couldn't read a word of it.
But it's something dry to sit on
when the rocks are damp.

My dormitory is exposed,
nights are cold, and from my kneeler
as I pray, or pretend to, I see
distant cities burning.
Humans are greedy, ignorant,
and violent,
also quite ordinary.

God was annoyed with humans.
He sent me out to teach them manners.
I gave classes, lectures, and symposia,
but among my students
I saw such lust for self-abasement,
such devotion
to the ludicrous and noxious,
that I despaired.
I was as unpersuasive as a parrot.
Man went on as he always did.
I'd done my best, but failed.
I tore my hair and left town.

I was homeless, socially inept,
and spiritually churlish.
I had a cloak of rough sacking,
hemp, with twigs imbedded,
and rope shoes. Nothing else.
No halo. I found a cave.
It's as dark as the Savior's tomb
before what's-his-name the angel
rolled the stone away.

But I'd saved some candle stubs
from my missionary days
and with these I could read a page or two
from *le Monde* each night.
The obit page, style,
premier league play.
I am grateful
when the raven brings fresh news,
good or bad no matter,
just words to read.

I have the oddest thoughts.
They're like the drops of melted glass.
God's tears. They glow.
I fear I'm mad.

When I blow the candles out,
my cave is lightless,
but it's not half so dark
as the human heart.
My demons come.

IX

They flit about my cave like circus bats.
They tell grave-yard jokes.
I laugh out loud,
or sneeze,
which clears off the bouts I have,
in spring especially,
of *congestion religieuse*,
though it might be pollen.

My demons are honest,
impudent, and practical.
I need them to untie the knots
in my tangled spirit
and to lace up my shoes.
I am getting older
and don't easily bend over.

Sometimes things seem better.
And yet when I saw the Chariot of Fire
with Elijah riding in it, raving
about being God's Chosen,
I understood that things
won't get better. That's
the truth of the matter.

Truth is God's gift
when He's got naught left to give.
I accept it, the little thing it is,
and here I offer it to you
and you.
I will offend some,
but don't blame me,
blame Him.

When I sleep,
I welcome dreams,
the more terrible the better,
because then my demons
can display their smarts.
I'm an eager pupil,
but old and fragile,
so I am thankful
that they are so careful
with my person.
They don't tell me everything
and for this I'm grateful.

We have adventures.
We fly above a world that was,
a world of sparkling streams
and sweet green grass,
a world inhabited by nature's
best creatures, the solid bison,
the clever fox, industrious beaver,
rodents by the thousands,
the lark and lizard.

As we fly, my demons hold me gently
in their ancient claws.
We drift, without a thought,
without a plan or prospects,

and there, below,
I see my ancestral village,
the women spreading sheets
along the river bank to bleach.
It's the sun-blessed land I knew

X

and loved, where I lived
before I discovered Death
and went off to indulge my flesh,
but then to discipline it severely,
needing, as every body does,
to have a calling.

Sainthood's mine.
But I've suppressed my hopes
for living's sake.

There's bird song in the willows.
The women are young and pretty.
They look up, smile, and wave.
Of their thighs, their ankles, and knees
I am tenderly and passionately
aware. I ask my demons
to carry me closer.

Thirteen ways of looking at God

Lines composed after a visit to
St. Pancras International rail station, London

The blackbird whirled in the autumn winds.
It was a small part of the pantomime.

Wallace Stevens

1.
I flew all night, out of Boston,
admiring the great engines that dragged me
over the dark cold water.
Me and my meager gear,
traveling light, myself at 200 pounds,
bags at 20, books that I never read in flight,
but think it better to be prepared
in case we crash, but have somehow managed
to be cushioned by a pinewoods and survive.
Where would that be?
Newfoundland?
I'd want a book to read
while awaiting rescue.

Or we've run out of fuel
and can't reach USAF Thule, Greenland,
something to distract me while we're going down.
But I am delivered safely,
and give thanks to God,

2.
or to the gods,
which ever or how many
were involved.
I am not a good flyer
and am grateful to all who helped.

3.
I lug my baggage, my books
and useless knowledge,
into the maze of the London Underground.
The Lord is my shepherd;
He unfolds my map.
I search out St. Pancras Station.
I've a train to catch.

4.
I think of him,
the boy called Pancras,
each time I take the train from here.
He deserves a memorial surely,
something muted, lit dimly,
and somewhere better than these littered
and cavernous halls, its pubs
full of yobs too beer-sodden to give a toss
about a boy who had his head lopped off.
"Believe what I say to believe,"
said Diocletian to the boy.
"My many divinities, young man,
not your one big God."
Diocletian was strict. An emperor:
no talking back.

God's responsible for all this,
He's responsible for what happens everywhere.
For Diocletian, for Pancras,
for my plane arriving safely and on time.
My train too seems on schedule,
so again I'm grateful.

5.
Pancras believed,
took Jesus as his scout master,
would not renounce
and that spelled disaster.

Pancras was the same age
as my grandson, fourteen,
when he lost his head.
I mean Pancras.
My grandson still has his.

6.
Would I have defied Diocletian?
Not likely. I couldn't obey
an emperor, or God either,
without a head,
or even cross the street.
I hate the idea of death.
I always hold my breath
'til the wheels touch ground.

7.
But would I defy God
or let Him down?
I would and often have.
Look now how I am,
afflicted with mild despair,
perpetual solitude,
and skeptical,

XI

8.
and now with shame for having lost
a universe, the one
I myself have made, the poems, and notes for poems,
the entire goddam thing,
while waiting on the outbound platform,
and distracted doubtless
by a pretty girl,
some boys filched it.
My overstuffed valise.
They rummaged through it
as they ran. I chased them,
muttering, not shouting
"stop, thief," which
would have been embarrassing.
I watched them dodging black cabs
on Euston Road, gleeful,
and I saw them cast my bag aside.
Just worthless papers
they surely thought.
By ignorance was thus saved
my inner life,
or, at least, all evidence thereof,
and since God's hand
is present in every random thing,
I took this as a message
that my poems were good enough,
at least for Him.

9.
I was restored.
I sat on an iron bench
and read a pamphlet that explains it all,
Einstein's bit, and some others,
concerning particles and such.
Another pamphlet told about Saint Pancras.

His name means
"he who holds everything;"
he's the saint of luggage then.

He protects against false witness,
headaches, and menstrual cramps,
all easy chores.
But for the terrible times we're in
there must be something more
that he can do. I pray, then,
not to God, but to Pancras
who is closer, naive, and easier
to implore.
Save us, I say, from liars
and bad people.

10.
As the station clock struck eleven
I nodded off – the flight across the Atlantic was long
and I'm exhausted –
I dreamt that I saw young Pancras
 in his Roman soldier's suit,
with a wooden sword and shield.
He was cheerful
and for the moment my dismal cloud
of *what's the point?* was lifted.
A true miracle!
Fine boy, like my grandson, fourteen.
I'm saved from psychotherapy again.

11.
Pancras, sainted, and in pieces,
came to Canterbury in a box marked "relics."
It was the baggage of Augustine,
brave Archbishop, sent in the year of Our Lord

five hundred and ninety seven
to convert the blue-faced Britons,
hooligans who'd never heard
of Jesus, the chieftain of the better people.
Augustine was eloquent and, besides,
he had what God provided for the trip,
not bright trinkets, but the magic bones.

12.
I went to Canterbury,
that reliquary of reliquaries.
In the British Isles, the place where most likely
you'd find evidence of God. (The station
is Canterbury West, *CBW* in BritRail speak,
Margate Sands is at line's end,
beyond which is *nothing*.)
I left on the 13:37.
I'd be at the cathedral by evensong.
I'd promised that I'd meet with Pancras in a pew,
catch up with him and Him.
I closed my eyes. In my dozing head
I heard the cosmic background buzz
of the big Rolls Royce engines,
wonders of moving parts,
that hung, improbably,
from the Boeing's wings and did not fall off.
These sounds soothed my soul.
I looked out the window,
saw England fly past,
saw a flight of blackbirds,
and a herd of cows. As to God,
I looked and looked.
I untied my shoes.

13.
But the bones, the bits and ribs,
tibias and femurs, none thick or long,
a boy no longer,
(all being disconnected,)
were either misplaced
in Canterbury's labyrinth of catacombs,
or, more likely, lost
on a selling trip among the savages.
They are, perhaps, in an old leather trunk
on a rusting rack in left-luggage,
bottom of the stairs, third door right.
There are rooms and corridors
that no one has visited
since King Henry's time.
But where *really* are Pancras' bones?
God only knows. As to the skull,
the perfidious Italians kept it.

How Fast the River Rose

How fast the river rose!
Up the water came,
past the East India Docks,
past Wapping and Saint Katherine's,
past the Isle of Dogs,
past Greenwich
with its pendulum and clocks.

It was a record tide,
the highest since Pepys
reported Whitehall quite drowned.
I heard the river. It sighed
and sung its dirge,
its epic slosh
against the pilings of the dock.

The river's swollen,
but I found a bridge that would take me
to the other side.
A one-legged man wanted coins
to let me pass.
I dropped a shilling in his cap.
"My other leg," he said,
"is in the Falklands.
I left it on a windy ridge
or on a gravel beach
for the gulls to eat."

At dark he climbs five flights
to his garret flat.
It takes an hour to climb.
He has no woman,
no canary, and no dog.

He writes poems,
one each night, poems about
old trollop Thames,
poems about the tides,
the birds that bob
like corks on the oily flood.
And about the royal barge
that carried kings and willing ladies
upstream to Hampton Court.
He imagines
that he had been an oarsman
in a life long past,
pulling against the current
while the music played.
Oar dip and splash,
gliding past the South Bank stews
and Master Shakespeare's Globe,
bumping now and then
against a floating corpse.

He cooks his dinner
on a cheap electric cooker,
winds his clock,
and pens his poems by candle light.

"Sweet Thames," he wrote,
"run softly until the world ends,
but before it does

let me have a woman just one more time.
That, or let my life be short."
I went down his creaking five-flight stair
holding to the rail lest I fall.
I walked into the London night.
I watched the running lights of tugs
and the ripple of the moon
on the river's darkling sheen.
I tasted ancient fog.

I walked along Embankment to St. Paul's.
I heard a noise through a metal grate.
The river, I thought, its song not over,
perhaps it sings to me.
But it was more a rumble than a song,
the Underground, the Central Line,
on its way to Bank
and Bethnal Green.

A Poem about Everything Disguised as a Poem about Poetry

From a crowded bus
I watched the world flutter past.
It disassembled
like an unstitched book.
Was it London where I rode,
or Jerusalem?
Or here, alas, at home?

I saw a ruined bridge.
I saw a city burning on a hill.
I saw bonfires built of books.
It was a butcher's moon,
dark red, and old.
The Temple stood dark
and empty, still unbuilt.
In ancient times I had come on foot,
now I come by bus.
Was I late, come just after,
or had I come too soon?

I inhaled poetry
from this troubled air.
I mistook a word here
and another there,
but most seemed sad and plain,
words like afraid
or lost
like shamed
or broken
words with meanings always
unmistakable.
Always clear.

I caught them up
as they floated past,
and put them
into ordered lines,
just as grammar advises.

Lines sometimes elusive,
but lucid always,
with no deceptions,
no surprises, accurate,
as only a map can be,

to remind me
of where we've been,
that names the bridge,
the date it fell,
its height above the river,
how many died,
the where it happened,
but never why.

I'll gather up the pages
and rebind the book.
Lest we forget,
lest we forget thee,
O world entire,

lest the avenging angel
drop his sword,
lest justice stumble
and drop her scales,
lest my words be scattered
by the storm.

IV

Florida, unkindly

Tropic air has music in it,
and palms with their fingered fronds
play rattling chords.
It's the sound that skeletons make
when they sit down or stand.

The clouds move slowly by.
There is no hurry.
In Florida, the days come and go,
and come around again
so often that no one notices.

Vultures, like children's kites,
hang suspended
above the ordered grid of towns
with their lawns trimmed down
to the dark-earth quick.

In Florida, the preacher says,
God's kingdom doth increase,
as does the mold between the walls,
I add, and the cold-sweat terrors
of old age and debt.

As the sun goes down,
bats emerge
from beneath a rusted bridge.
They scatter bravely
to the insect wars.
The mosquitoes do not surrender
and their kingdom also
doth increase.

In Florida, emptiness
is what everyone most fears.
Death knocks upon our doors just once,
but emptiness comes down the street
each morning, with his noisy little blower.
He herds the fallen leaves
and cuttings along the road,
and next morning, sends them back,
starts over.

Automobiles move
like flocks of robotic sheep.
They surge and stop,
then surge again
when the light turns green.
They seem angry
or confused.

Flickering blue light
leaks out of windows
and pollutes the night.
In Florida, all is neon after dark,
pink and purple,
or stark white in tubes
that hum as the universe
is said to do.

The ocean slowly rises.
But no worries, dear,
we'll be gone
ere downtown floods.

Easter Sunday:
The Circus Comes to Town

The churches are abuzz today.
The organs play martial music.
Onward Christian Soldiers
is the favorite of the crowd.
The calliopes join in.
The circus has come to town.

The barkers in white robes and funny hats
mount their pulpits to declaim,
pronounce, and huckster.
The pulpit is a soap box;
any brand will do, so long as
it proclaims itself as new, improved,
and that the soul gets whiter.

Sparky clean these barkers are
and perfumed
with scent of myrrh to hide
the fear of ending up as meal
for worms or rats,
or worse than death, an afterlife
of being lectured at.
Which among them
has not sinned or strayed?
So many choices the church provides,
sodomy, gluttony, luxury,
or having doubts
about the business that they're in.

But this holy morning
the dawn comes in like pink spun sugar,
and the world's reborn in big-top splendor.
Overnight, the camels came
with cartons of soft drinks,
and sacks of peanuts in their shells.

And lions also came.
On Seconal, and Placidyl,
they're quite tame.
They romped among delighted children
and ate not one.

Facsimiles of the holy martyrs
in plaster and bright paint
line the midway.
Come see, the barkers call.
We've got your favorites.
Lawrence on his barbeque,
Stephen the walking pincushion
tranced out in the sun,
and look, here's Agatha
with her breasts on a silver plate,
and the blessed Magdalene
who hasn't bathed in years.

And there are gifts eternal
for the nippers,
plastic toys that never break
no matter how violent
the brat becomes.
There's Godzilla,
Cinderella, Action Heroes
in tight pants and shirts,

and, in synthetic plush,
the last white rhinoceros on earth.

Great Zeus
and the entire Olympian crew
appear as freaks,
kept on the bill as bait for gawkers;
eight francs the front row seats,
three francs for standing.

At last, the Wonder Boy,
the one we've come to see,
appears as *artiste de trapéze*.

Has He come back
to judge this miserable mob of us?
We wait and sweat and trepidate.
Such a pathetic band of frauds we are,
thugs and liars and hypocrites,
the avaricious in their tailored suits,
the vacuous, the incurious, the bored.

But no, it's not Judgement Day,
not yet. Today's just show.

Come see, the barkers call, *come see*
how the Savior keeps his Balance
between the Living and the Dead.
He treads a wire invisible
stretched between
two tortured eucalyptus trees,
while below, on this very circus ground,
the thieves go free.

XII

Hunting Day

On hunting day,
the wives to church in Sunday best.
In pews they sit and pray to Jesus,
Mary, Saint Hubert too,
to keep their husbands safe
as they hunt the boar,
safe from sprains and falls,
from excess drink,
and from accidental shootings
of each other.

The dogs,
happy to be running free,
bellow, bark, and holler,
but aren't much use.
Meanwhile, *Sanglier*,
the dark lord of the thorny brush,
settles into some mottled shade
and keeps the huntsmen stumbling
on the distant hill
in view.

Morning in the Languedoc

Mistral's gentle daughter
awakens in her bed of lavender
and watches night recede.
The stars are vanishing.
She has no walls or windows.
She sleeps *plein air.*

Her father is a big fellow.
He lives in a mountain grotto,
keeps untamed horses,
and pounds on drums.
Today, though, he sleeps in.

Her breath stirs the poplars
and the olives. The leaves rustle.
The cypress in the yard,
a column that holds up the sky,
is strong as marble,

but now it sways,
and, oh so slightly, bends.
Matins, far off.
The bell tolls, six faint strokes
in a minor key.

The sun, all night hidden
in abandoned houses
of remote Vaucluse, comes out.

Mistral's daughter
has promised bird song
and it begins. Her breath
is sometimes sweet as butterflies,
but sometimes acrid,
sharp with smoke
from vineyard prunings,
twigs and branches smoldering
between the rows.

Now light, in particles,
like pollen shaken from the trees,
flows into the valleys
and along the sandy banks
of the mighty Rhone.

Mount Ventoux, beyond the river,
is sculpted against a sky so clear
that we almost forget
that it ever rains. When it does,
the windows streak because
the road outside is dust.

The sky was old
before the day began.
The sky is always old,
but sunlight,
as it falls upon the land,
is new each day.

The waters of the river gleam
coppery and green,
like the bronze of a Roman sword
pulled out last Tuesday
from the river's mud.

In the orchard down the path,
a chainsaw sputters into life
and whines. The tree will fall
and be gone by noon.
The tree was old
and much battered by Mistral,
who is even older.
Great winds on earth
as there are in heaven.

Across the stubbled field
and down our dead-end road,
the lame rooster crows.
It is his job
to announce the dawn.

Behind the limestone wall,
the mastiffs, their night-time noise
and nonsense done, snort and snuffle
and find some shade.
The heat begins.

Mistral's daughter brings
the scent of lavender
in her tattered basket.
She apologizes
for the rooster's rustic manners.
And for the rude dogs too.

The magpies chatter.
The sun rolls up the sky
on burning wheels.

XIII

My Life with Homer: Pigalle

Last Tuesday evening,
waiting for the bus, corner
rue Martyrs and Saint Lazare,
my head full of car exhaust and Homer,
I was thinking
about Apollo's rustled cattle,

and about the sirens
who sang such lovely songs
that a man must tie himself
to a telephone pole or mast
lest he dive heedless
into a raging sea.

And thus distracted,
I stepped into the path
of the very bus I waited for,
the *soixante-sept.*

The 67, that storied bus.
It shuttles seekers, the spiritually confused,
and the occasional office worker
between the sacred and profane.
Notre Dame, the shrine to Our Blessed Lady,
is one terminus;
Place Clichy, the other,
domain of ladies of the *rue.*

The journey, from Paris 4 to Paris 9
and back again, is perilous.
Take care, the philosophers advised,
lest your head be fuddled.

But too late received, that council.
I'd tasted the bright neon-honey
of the dark nocturnal.
I sought self-knowledge,
with, perhaps, some small adventures
on the side.

It was on this quest
that I was almost run over.
It was dusk.
The driver found the brake in time.
Putain d'idiot, the driver yelled.
A nasty blow to my self-regard.
The faces at the windows,
mortals going home from work,
saw not a man on the hero's journey,
but a *putain d'idiot, moi.*

Embarrassed, I retreated.
I'd been saved – temporarily at least –
I caught the next.

At Pigalle, the fountain, turned off for winter,
was full of floating trash.
There were nymphs and satyrs,
and always are, winter,
summer, and between.
The satyrs, disguised
as teenaged boys,
were picking pockets.
I pretended to be a writer.
I would make some notes.

I found a bench, cleaned my glasses,
and took out my pen.
The satyrs lost interest;
I had nothing
but a plastic pen to steal.

Then Debauchery, herself, the muse,
appeared and took my hand.
Nymphs, wearing skirts too short for winter
and wrapped in tattered boas,
bored but faithful, waited in the doorways
for the likes of me.

I'd been saved, it seemed,
from death by bus
for adventures in the demi-monde.
And to write a poem.
This night is likely, so I began it,
to be long and the tides are strong,
and I'm still alive.
But why, I asked myself,
to take the trip back safely down,
not waste a round-trip ticket?

Night descended.
Place Clichy at rush-hour
is waves of headlights churning;
the maelstrom of Charybdis
plays nightly in the Paris 9th.
Then the beautiful Calypso,
yes, herself, in black mesh stockings
and stiletto heels, reached out
pulled me from the surf.

She leaned against a lamp post,
the classic pose.
The post transformed
into a footman with a sputtering lantern.
Particles of light fell around her
and settled in her hair.
She spoke and I was bewitched,
or, better said, ensnared.

What will I become if I stay too long?
But I knew.
A pathetic figure,
gaunt and wasted, lost forever.
I saw opium in that future,
the pipe handed me
by the ghost of Charles Baudelaire.
Or a tormented moralist.
Or posturing and self-deceived,
a *faux* anthropologist.
Some sort of nocturnal creature,
hence pale.

Could I listen to the sirens singing
and not drown?
Could I save myself?

I reached out, as if to a buoy of cork,
and grabbed more practical questions.
How exactly
did Hermes avoid the wrath
of his older, bigger, brother?
My cattle, you brat! Apollo raged.
Charm, I think, saved him,
and his wits.

My life with Homer: Rosie

for Ellen

I call my sweetheart Rosie.
She slips from bed,
puts delicate feet in slippers
and flings the windows wide.
With the sun not quite risen,
she, subtle as the dawn,
slips back into the bed
and wakes me.
We leave the curtain open.

The petals of the morning
are scattered on our bed.
On the window sill
the red geranium in a pot
announces morning
with the brio of a rooster.
Rosie disperses
the nightmarish cobwebs
from the rafters of my soul.
"Have better dreams,"she says,
"and you'll live longer."

Rosie arranges flowers in a vase.
She tends our garden.
The iris in the spring,
are purple, violet, and blue.
She paints the morning sky
with slender fingers,
pinks and yellows,

XIV

and a touch of rose.
As my muse, she keeps me honest.
No lies, no puffery, no pretense.
She keeps our lives from falling
into disarray.

I have disquiets that Rosie calms.
She applies a balm distilled
from bee's wax, moonlight,
and a splash from the wine dark sea.

I love her legs, her thighs, and knees.
Her arms are white as Aphrodite's were,
and her ankles better.
She keeps the embers glowing
in my heart. It's no wonder
that I gave up adventuring
and came home.

The Pilgrim

The tale of human kind
exhausts my mind.
Which way does God
suggest we go? And which way
is Spain? And then

I heard a flock clattering
down the mountain trail,
through the dry oak forests
along the hard tracks
of flint and slate,

and I heard their shepherd,
a girl,
telling stories to the sheep,
words in sing song
to ease their fear of wolves.
And she promised water.
The hot day nearly over.

She caressed the simple hearts
of her animals.
When they came upon the patch
of forest where I rested,
they were not afraid.

"Have no fear of him,"
I heard her say,
"He's a pilgrim.
He's lost God
and thinks he'll find Him
in some old bones."

I have a gourd of stale water
hanging from my neck
and my pouch is empty,
not a bean or coin in it.
But my heart is pure.
I have my faith,
my devotion to the Lord's favorite,
the Apostle James
the Elder.

The shepherdess gave me shelter
in her barn. Night gathered.
I watched her fingers
coax milk from an ewe's udder.
She filled a red clay cup
with warm milk, drank from it,
then gave the rest to me.
It was my first supper
in a thousand years.

She freshened the water
in my gourd
and spread clean straw.
I lay down with the slumbering flock.
Sheep sleep standing.
I had not known.

I did not sleep well.
In the night my heart flamed up
and in that light
I saw myself and knew
that I'd not be again
the man I'd always been.
I knew that I must leave
lest the straw ignite.

As the sun came up,
I searched out the road.
Which way to go?
I saw dust in each direction.
She watched me from the window.
She shook her bedclothes
and flakes of the night flew off
like the seeds of the willow tree.

Her arms are slender,
graceful, strong.
Her skin is smooth as river pebbles.
She is neither white nor dark.
A girl of the desert,
no Christian either.

Can the Holy Book
explain the forest,
the stories told
to a dog and sheep,
or the parable of the heart afire,
or the sharing of a cup?

A Mountain in the Midi

How fast the disturbance came on
as I drove south,
not the rain that we so needed,
but it was time itself
that seemed undisciplined,
as if returning
to the place it came from.
The road turned toward the lowering sun
and I was briefly blinded,
as if I'd tripped on a root and fallen.
But I caught myself,
and just at the road's edge,
the precipice,
I stopped the car.

The air, the light
seemed from elsewhere,
but I felt present.
I listened to cicadas
chanting in the forest.
They'd pause and start over,
like holy men counting beads.

From the road's edge
the land fell away,
a steep decline into a bottomless tangle
of gaunt oaks, boulders,
thorns, and brush.

Beyond were layers of mountains,
hills, and canyons,
their shapes shifting
as the sun went down and shadows lengthened.
A particular mountain emerged,
a mountain I was sure
I'd seen before, but long ago.

A limestone ridge, this mountain,
its flanks scoured
by winds carrying tiny blades
of silica and quartz,
its body cracked by freeze and thaw,
by the furious heat
of the southern summer,
by repeated violations
of insistent roots,
and by exhausting months
of cloudless skies,
with neither shade nor rain.

Then, as I gazed,
the mountain seemed to stir,
an effect of the fading light perhaps,
and the August air, a shimmer;
and now I saw a woman sleeping,
lying on her side.
I recognized this woman.
I recognized the hillock of her head,

then another, a bit higher,
of her shoulder, then the curve
of waist and hips, her thighs,
a ravine defining the space between,
her slender legs that sloped down
to the plain below, to a land
of towns and roads,
power lines, farms, and rails.

What do you look at so intently?
someone might have asked.
There's nothing there,

and I'd have said
that I knew this mountain long ago,
that I had loved her,
and on the 979 today,
coming south from Vallons,
a great truth overcame me,
a sudden turbulence
of light and joy,
of sorrow too,
for I'd gone off to find the world,
and I'd lost her, forgotten
who she was and where.
But then, at a turning of the road,
she was there. Older,
but I loved her still,
and I knew that I would love her
as I had before,
love the steep slopes
and dried up springs,
the crevasses and fissures,
the ravines and rocks.

As the sun withdrew,
night came on.
I stayed a while longer.
I watched the moon arrive,
watched the mountain sleeping.
I knew its quiet heart was beating,
one pulse each ten thousand years.

The Midi is the French term for the south of the country, Provence and Occitanie.

XV

Cabbage Soup

Cabbage soup is a blending,
a nebulous mixing,
pleasant enough at creation,
easily digestible;
we always liked it.
But when the dark earth
that the cabbage grew in
is added for grit
or for color
it becomes another experience
altogether.

The soul of a cabbage
is an overlapping
of convolutions
in which can hide
an almost infinite number
of variations, coriander, for instance,
tomatoes, carrots, religions,
and garlic, notions
and superstitions, turnips
and potatoes, predictions,
celery, ambitions and envy,
spite, ground pepper,
hatreds, the numberless stars
in their heavenly placements,
the goat and the bull,
the crab and the bear,
the dog, unruly clusters

of gases, vapors bubbling,
a dash of vinegar,
gravitational attraction,

and all this has simmered so long
that the ingredients no longer
differentiate,
and we've been left
with a soup that's as unknowable
and unrepeatable
as it is unforgettable.
A wonder,
almost indigestible.

But we sit down to it daily,
as worshipers do at an altar.
We'd die without it.

Meanwhile, below stairs,
the chef, who's as blind
as the Great Sphinx of Giza,
stumbles about wondering
where his wife went
and with whom.
Didn't he notice?
Feckless. Careless
it turns out,
so things fell apart,
and everything is still falling
the ovens the sinks
the hooks the drains
the menus the napkin holders;

but we, the lucky ones
still alive, are oblivious
and sit down to what always
might be our last supper.
Meanwhile,

a great commotion outside;
as we always do, we run out to see.
It's an overturned farm cart,
the chickens running loose,
going every which way.
There's a crow
on the telegraph wire.
And the wheel of the cart
is still turning, a lazy continuation
of collisions and cataclysms,

meanwhile, the soup in our bowls
is getting cold
as we stand at the roadside
                                        gawking

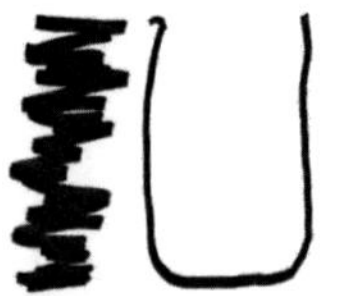

VI

The Hindu Poems

for Satyajit Ray
without whose poetic vision I'd know nothing of India

XVI

Life is a Homespun

Life is a tattery thing
said my mother,
not a pattern in it
and stitched poorly.
The sari of your grandmother
has more of the mind in it.

My father says
it's like a patchwork bedcover,
but one stitched together
by the ants.

I spent my childhood climbing trees.
With my friends I watched armies
traversing the plains.
Great clouds of dust rose
as men and animals
marched back and forth.
The vultures circling overhead
were like kites
and we boys held the strings.
The vultures tugged at us.
We danced, laughed,
and were jerked about.

When I was twelve
I watched the girls of our village
as they sat at their spindles,
their delicate fingers

moving swiftly,
neither ahead of time
nor behind it.
I was in love with a girl
who worked at a loom.
I never knew what name to call her.
Her employer was unrelenting.
I loved and I suffered.
As a young man
I learned that the self,
with its suffering,
is a delusion.
The self knows only itself,
and never understands
that it is nothing.

Ganges is eternal.
It teems with sacred bacteria.
Indra freed the waters from the mountains
to make the dry land green.

I will grow into my assigned place
in this kingdom of the gods
and of vultures. In the city,
there are motorbikes dashing about,
screaming and spewing smoke.
No one is ever on time.
I will go to the city
when I am a man.

XVII

Nandi and the Goddess

Lord Shiva ties his bull calf
to the threshing post.
Blessed Nandi, his horns just sprouted,
his white body is as smooth
as velvet soaked in milk.
Round he goes, trampling the wheat.
The wind from the yellow plains
carries the chaff away and kernels remain.
The birds come. They are greedy.
The village children,
little creatures with bare feet,
prance about,
shrilling their bamboo flutes,
and chase them off.

In the courtyard,
under the sprawling and rustling leaves,
in the beautiful shade,
sits Parvati, the beautiful goddess.
Round and beautiful breasts,
her beautiful navel.
Parvati, beloved of Shiva.

The music of pomegranates
chimes in my ears.
Magpies have drifted down
from the foothills of the great range.
They chatter, telling stories
of their distant homeland.

Parvati is beautiful.
The magpies bring gifts,
glass beads red as pigeon blood,
silver chains they have stolen.

And ambassadors have come.
They spread rich carpets on the ground,
carpets patterned with lotus blossoms,
with peacocks in many colors,
with blue elephants.

They kneel on the carpets
and Parvati receives them.
She lifts her right leg,
puts her foot on the ledge.
She opens her heart and her loins.
With spoons carved from a bull's horn
the ambassadors spill seed
into her sacred womb.

Pomegranate juice
dribbles down my chin.
Parvati the beautiful,
my beloved.

The twenty-six ambassadors
said not an intelligible word.
They come from foreign lands,
beyond the ranges.

Lord Shiva is glad that his wife is with child.
Nandi is happy. The grain is good.
Tonight we will chase away the demons.

They will hide in the forest
and disguise themselves as monkeys,
spoiled little princelings
with fur on their bottoms.

The Jacaranda Tree

The mother Jacaranda of our village,
its leaves, branches,
and beautiful flowers,
holds light longer
than does the earth
or the forests.
Light drains out of the stones,
out of the walls
and the wells,
but in the trees
there is still the trembling
of gentle violet,
of the beautiful flowers.
Then there's the dark purple
of the coming darkness,
then indigo blackness,
then the sacred blackness
of burnt cattle bones.

The Jacaranda's perfume lingers
in the warm night.
It is like the sweet smell
of the village cattle.
When the traders come
we sell the straw the cattle have pissed in,
and the traders sell it
to the makers of yellow.

It is spring.
In the day time,
when mother Jacaranda is in bloom,
happiness surrounds us.

Bones and horns of cattle
are scattered in the fields.
I gather them up and carry them
in woven bags.
The bags are of hemp
that scratch my bare legs.

I leave the bones
at the temple of lord Vishnu.
The priests make medicines and charms
and they give me food.

In the evening
I sit with my back to the tree.
Night surrounds me.
I watch the invisible owls
and listen to the silence of bats.
The breeze in the Jacaranda
whispers the sacred Vedas
and Vishnu is pleased.

When I lie down to sleep
I put my ear to the ground.
I can hear the carts
drawn by the white bullocks,
the wooden wheels rumble
and the axels squeak.
The sound that the sun makes
as it descends is different.
Twilight has a sound like a brass bowl
being rubbed with a rabbit skin.

Ferry Sinking

After the storm had passed
small waves whispered
against the shingle.
The ferry will not come,
the water said; it has sunk.
Flotsam and life-rings wash up,
and then bodies
of mothers and grandmothers
of sons and daughters.
The bodies of workers
but without their tool bags.
Their hammers, trowels, and chisels
are at the bottom of the bay.

Funerary fires blossom
up and down the beach.
One hundred eighty-three have died.
What did I see? the official asks.
I saw the Lord Vishnu walking
along the surface of the waves.
With his broom
he swept his drowned children
toward the shore.

Vishnu has many arms and hands.
He holds a flower and the hammer,
the broom, the trowel and the chisel,
the typhoon, and the thunder.

Not all mishaps can be averted,
Lord Vishu has said.
But the universe will be saved.
This much he has promised.

Plague Times: 2020

Traces of death smoke
come in the window.
It's spring, and we'd left it open.
We are educated people,
come down from the capital,
fleeing the foul air.
But here too there is the pestilence.
I press my forehead to the window frame.
"Kama has deserted us,"
my lover says.

The smell of the cremation pyres
woke her. The death count rises.
The street noises begin.
Roosters, motorbikes, hawkers,
donkeys carrying bundles of firewood
for the pyres. The donkeys
are patient and faithful.
They have not deserted us.
Their little feet clicking on the stones,
delicate, are like rain drops
on a drum head.

Vishnu Warned Us

Man is the rat that gnaws
through the sack
and gorges himself.
There is no grain for the future.

Man is a moth that makes holes
in the fabric of heaven.
He is the hole maker,
the careless one.

But I am an old man now.
I sit beneath the banyan tree.
I scratch my sores
and I study scripture.

What the words mean is a mystery.
I trace the beautiful letters
with my finger. Lord Vishu
appeared to me
in a dream, and lingers.

VII

Going to See the Oracle

XVIII

The Frog

Her dog is tied to the tree. The bus pulls up. The bus driver helps us down. He wears a cape of wolf fur over his shoulders and on his bald head, a khaki colored cap with a badge. A snake, embroidered in gold, twines around a staff; the field is indigo. Stars are suggested by white flecks, but this might be dust. The road to the mountain top is dirt. The dog begins to howl, animal terror, as if the earth were falling away. The driver throws the dog a biscuit and it lies down. We stand in the courtyard in the gravel and manure; somewhere there are donkeys. "The Oracle will see you," the driver says. I put my token in the slot and the door opens.

She is a presence, indeed, and has long been. She is seated on a lacquered wooden stool, red with gold leaf legs ending as paws of a lion. The fumes swirl around her, buzzing like kindly bees. She begins without preamble, without courtesies.

"I saw a large frog, swamp green, shiny and lumpy like a spoon of duck fat in a cold pan. The frog lay on its side, resting its ugly head in its four-toed hand."

Like the Buddha, I think, in a cave on the subcontinent. My expectations are high.

"Not like the Buddha," the oracle said, having read my thought, "before the Buddha, before even Elohim. I am older." You'd never guess. She looked great.

"The frog," the Oracle said, "wanted to become something

useful". I had dissected a frog in high school biology class. This was useful: I learned anatomy. "Kind of useful" the oracle said, apparently knowing everything that I thought. Very creepy, like the internet. "No," she continued, "something beautiful".

The frog wanted to be a lacquered breadbox or a ginger jar in porcelain, a delicate light green, celadon, smooth with no warts. Or perhaps even both. And so it did; it became a Ginger Jar, silent, dignified, its form calm and eternal. And it also became a Breadbox; the Breadbox speaks for them both.

This was the sort of thing I'd come for! Wonders. Duality. Both this and that. Jar out of Box, the Box and the Jar! I am suspended between utter disbelief and total belief. The oracle went on.

XIX

"The Breadbox announced that they wanted pocket money. Would they work for the money? I said that I needed help in the kitchen."

Another wonder! A woman, a high priestess, who is two thousand, three hundred and sixty years old who does her own cooking! She agreed. "I am a wonder," she said. Long legs crossed, a delicate ankle and slender foot ended the leg uppermost, the one crossed over the other, and she had a good tan despite long hours in a grotto. I was having inappropriate thoughts. "I am," she said, "everything you'd like to know." Things were becoming beyond surreal, unreal, *sous-le-reel.* Even flirtatious? This is ridiculous, I thought. Again, she knew my thoughts. "Better ridiculous than terrible," she said.

With rain strangeness often happens. "The Frog is the soul," the Oracle said, "ambiguous, amphibious. Previously a tad pole, now realized, and sacred to the gods."

In high school we had poked around in our dissected frog, saw the heart, the lungs and stomach. Saw no evidence of a soul, which was what I, already precocious in a philosophical way, was looking for.

"You must take your straw basket and cross the northern border. Fill it with all manner of precious medicines and return. Also bring back strips of papyrus with fragments of poems on them. I like Sappho, but the library's copy has been filched. Take some counterfeit coins as gifts for the natives. Go to their markets, their assemblies, their great events. They won't know a counterfeit from a counterfactual, a peanut from a pearl. That is all I have for today. Exit through the gift shop. Send in the next. Watch out for the dog."

XX

Sainte-Victoire and Hortense

"She don't do Mandarin," said M. Fiquet, "nor *teh Rooshin*." He smirked, as if to complement himself for his snide jab at Catherine's formerly great empire. But to be dismissive of Mandarin struck me as foolish. Half the persons on our tour bus were Chinese, travelling *ensemble*, many with umbrellas. There was a covey of American Pentecostals in the bus. "We're off to the Holy Land," the lady sitting next me in the bus revealed. She wore a name tag which I declined to read because it was pinned to her blouse at breast height.

"Some will say that she speaks only gibberish," continued M. Fiquet. He meant Pythia, the oracle. After two thousands plus years of useless prophecy, maybe she was just tired of talking.

I subject myself to tour-bus chit-chat as punishment for my innate snobbishness, an annoying know-it-all-ness. I am politically embarrassed by this side of myself, so the tour is a form of penance. Initially I came on tours because I'd been told that I'd meet interesting people, and save money too, but that seldom happened. The interesting people part, I mean. That's not to say that some weren't interesting to each other, but as a self-absorbed outlier, as a "thinker" as I like to think of myself, I was, mercifully, left out of the chit-chat loop.

Nevertheless, year after year, I do it. It's like Lent. I deprive myself of what I most need: solitude, intelligent conversation, wit. I come then as a pilgrim whose faith will be proven by the sacrifice. This year I wear the mask of "Heterosexual, Suitably Repressed." Next year, I'll come as somebody else. My being is in flux.

I often find myself standing in our group looking up at some building, listening to the guide, and feigning both interest and ignorance. Some woman of a certain age invariably attaches herself to me. I fend her off. I am committed to the Oracle.

M. Figuet wiggles his little flag. He is French. Last year the guide was Ms. Cormedoro, a Philippine doctorial candidate who dyed her hair red. The year before .... I have notes, but there is no need. In recent years the tourists have learned to take pictures of themselves with their phones held on the end of a long stick. On my first trip – oh so many years ago – most tourists had box cameras and had to advance the film with a knob. There was a window at the back of the camera through which you could see a number. By subtracting this number from twelve you knew how many more pictures you could take. Not many. There wasn't much to photograph. The temple was a ruin, as was every place.

How did this obsession of mine begin? Probably as most quasi-religious projects do: I had a vision. Mine arrived as a dream. There were jackals and vultures rummaging about in a jumble of bodies. It was like an after-the-action tableau in a Japanese samurai movie, smoking timbers and stone of what had been castles, horses wandering about riderless, their stirrups dangling and saddles empty, torn battle flags on broken staffs jabbed into the mud by the dying standard bearer. Pure Kurosawa. What struck me in the dream (I am a person in the dream, but a come-lately, out of costume) was the sheer number of the dead. It was as if the beast of the apocalypse had finally marched out on the plains and had had it out with itself. It was as if all the wars, the American Civil War, the Hundred Years War, The War of Spanish Succession, the Battle of the Somme, the Siege of the Alamo, the Trojan War had all happened at once.

Dreams may not be comprehensible, but they do tell a story. I was dismayed, horrified, but then I had the vision. At the perimeter of this smoldering catastrophe, a tall woman of a certain age, between 43 and 47 years, was walking. (In the dream, I have had police training so could make that sort of educated guess about her age.) She wore a toga in the Greek style, a bare shoulder, and with one hand she lifted the hem a few inches so that it not drag in the gore and dust.

She was beautiful, I could see her feet and her sandals, a thong was wrapped up the ankle to the calf. Miraculously her feet stayed clean. What under heaven matters as much as a woman's beauty? Her attitude, serene and aloof, seemed to say "I predicted this." "But that's easy," I thought in the dream, "because that's what you do. You're an oracle."

My adoration that was born that night. Now I was going to see her again, the oracle.

Delphi 67 km. Arrow to the left. The road wound upwards, hair-pin turns, goats on the rocky slopes, an occasional T shirt shop. My seatmate, whose name I steadfastly refuse to learn, engaged me. I glance at her tag. She is from "THE GREAT STATE OF ALABAMA." All caps. Alabama, I know from reading, is a primitive sub-country in the United States. How did she look, this lady? As pleasant as can be, round of face indicating good nutrition, no makeup or ornament except for the tag, skirt down to her shoe top.

M. Fiquet, at the front of the bus, droned on and on, like a salt mill operated by a dwarf with a hand crank.

"I speak in tongues," my seat neighbor goes on, "afmils coandant prebisois, aggga? do you think it possible the Oracle will understand me? Perhaps she and I can converse." *Sainted Christopher*, I say sotto voce, invoking the patron of travelers and protection-against-the-bad-trip, *help me*. "Or understand all of us together?" The thought of ten Pentecostals in the grotto talking in tongues at once... Perhaps M. Figuet would break the visits into subsets, timed entry, 2 French, 2 Dutch, 2 English, 2 Mandarin, 2 Pentecostals. I don't say "us' because I have always had the good sense to buy a single entry ticket, the premium, for a private audience. The real reason I've kept to the tours has been to save enough money to be able to buy the premium ticket.

Once, I remember, on one of my earliest pilgrimages, Pythia was not on her stool. Behind the stool was a black curtain. I dared to look behind it. There was a little kitchen, a kettle jiggling and puffing on a single burner gas ring, plastic bread box with a green lid, a vase with a geranium on the window sill. On the counter, a green ginger jar, with a repair, poorly glued. Out the window there was a familiar *paysage au plein air*, real air, real sky, and in the distance, the silhouette of Mount Sainte-Victoire. The oracle came in, never noticed me because we live on different planes, different dimensions. She was wearing blue denim cut-offs. Her legs long, graceful. Homer would have had an epithet for her, one based surely on her legs. She was tanned as only the Mediterranean sun can do, an ankle chain of yellow gold. She was a golden woman of a golden age of mankind, before devices, before shaved legs. There was a golden furze upon them. If I were Lesbian, a poet like Sappho, I would court her with poetry. But alas, I'm cursed with modernity and masculinity.

XXI

In the dream, I screwed up my nerve, approached her, crossing the mythos barrier, and asked, "How did the world come about?" I trembled, frightened by my presumption. I was asking the most fundamental question, the question of questions, whether in physics or theology. And I was asking about the past; her specialty was the future. She paused in her walk. A slight smile. She spoke in Greek, and the miracle of speaking tongues must have been at work, because I understood every word.

"You work with what you see before you," she said. "You have Sainte-Victoire and you have Hortense, a tree, and maybe some rocks. You make do." I awoke in a joyous sweat. I understood everything.

VIII

Marginalia

Bowl, no Spoon

On a wooden table
a white bowl. Steam rises.
There's no spoon.

A woman's voice.
Come, she says.

Is it my mother
and it's supper time?

Or my lover,
and we can let the soup get cold?

I may never know whose voice it is,
but the soup smells good,

and I'll find a spoon.

I watch the pollen blowing

I watch the pollen blowing
from tree to tree.

And I watch the little birds,
play the game.
The males in pursuit;
the ladies fluttery and coy.
From the thorny tangle of the hedge,
the ladies cry out "mate,
come mate with me.
Let us make more of us."

Such rage for procreation!
The pleading of birds
that must die by the hecatomb
to make room for still more birds.
They, in their turn, will fill the air
with that same sweet song,
"let us make more of us.
more and more, more of us."

The Sun like a Sailboat

The sun like a sailboat
scuds among the April clouds.
I am splashed
with light and shadow.

The new leaves flutter in the trees
like green butterflies.
In the sycamores, the jackdaws
are already nesting.

Lunch in the Midi

We will speak of death
at lunch, on the terrace,
while the cicadas in the dry pines
saw away on their fiddles.

Butterflies, like the hordes of Atilla,
ravage the fields of lavender,
but gently.

The Invention of the Roof

I
In eight or nine short cantos,
all science, all truthful,
a discourse on the common structures
which in pitch, composition,
and intention,
deflect the particles
that heaven sheds
as it decays,

II
and rain and hailstones as well.
God gets serious with hailstones

III
intending to strike down
the shameless who invariably shelter
beneath church porches,
the politicians and oligarchs,
get them as they're running
to and from their limos.

IV

A roof, whether of slate, tile, thatch,
or *la tôle ondulée* of tin that shelters minor beasts, like pigs,
that sleep, eat, and fornicate
just as we better beasts do

V
is a great invention,
adapted also to protect
the great libraries
that one needs to research
all sorts of things, the history
for instance, of roofs,
and to protect the diligent,
the scholar, or the conscientious parent
from the occasional cloud bursts
of silliness,

VI
as this poem is. Just six cantos,
as it turned out.

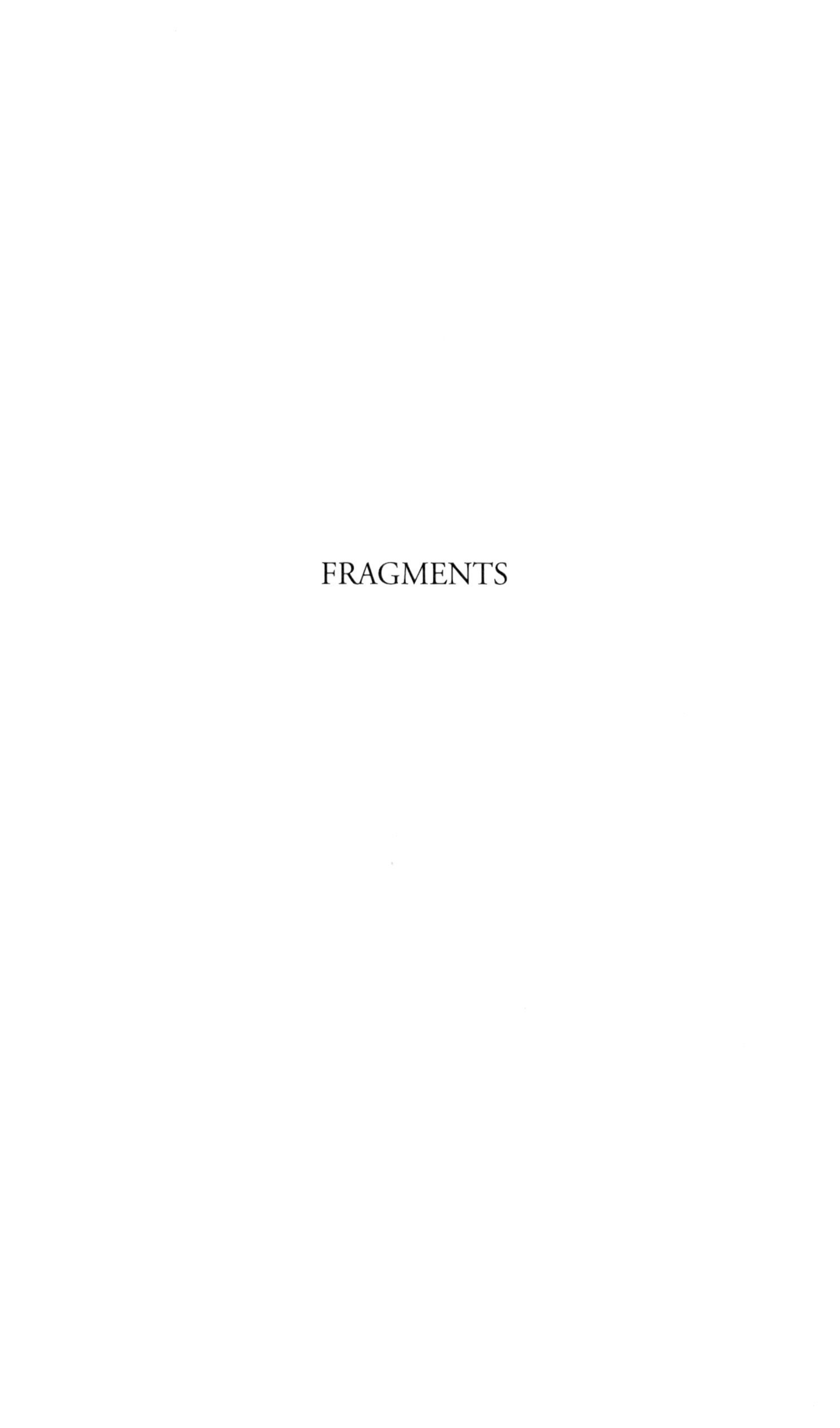

FRAGMENTS

Humans do not hear
the music of the spheres,
nor can we feel the rhythms
the gods live by.
The beating of our hearts
is too close, too loud,
too fast.

*

The sun moves upon its track
each day higher.
Spring at last.
I sit in outdoor cafes
beneath plane trees.
The leaves come out.
With light and shadow
I am dappled.

On my 83rd Birthday

My doctor has delicate hands.
She put a cold instrument to my chest
and announced that my heart
has miles yet to run,
joys to know, sorrows to bear.
But your dying, she said,
has now, alas, begun.

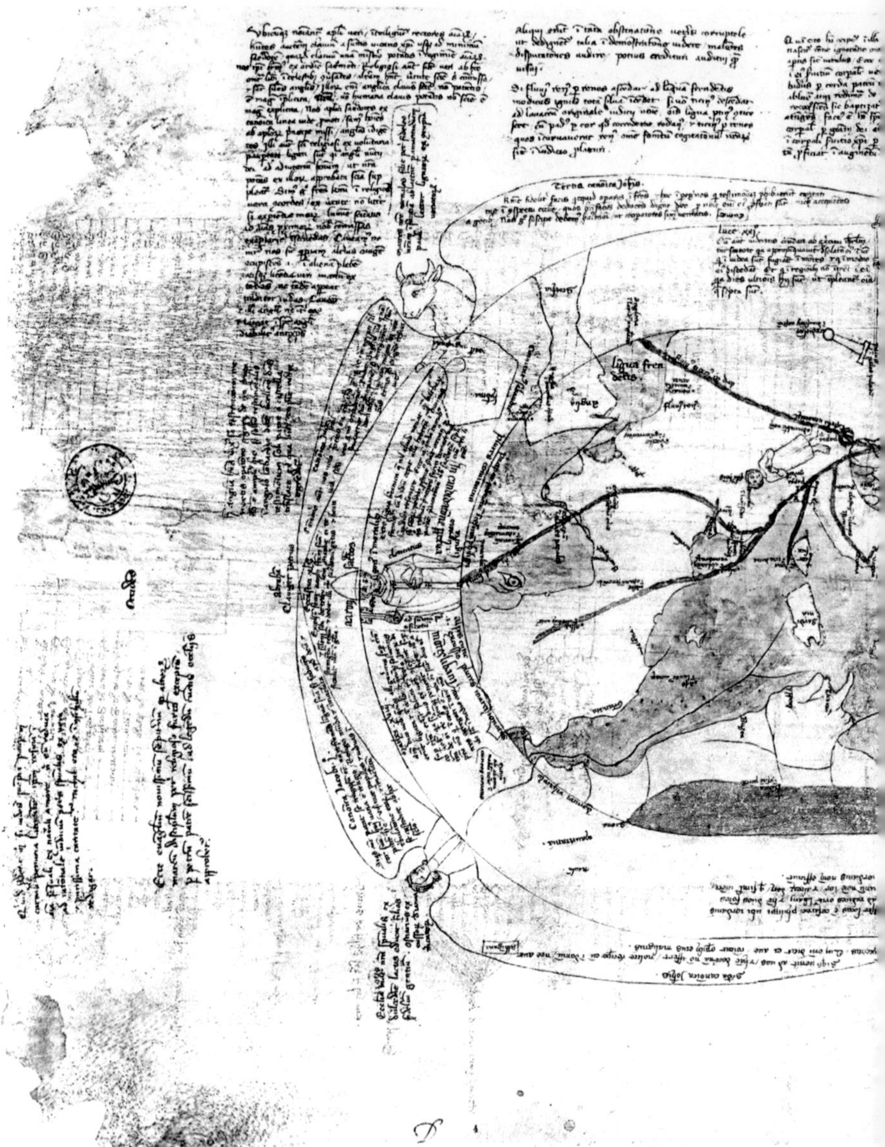

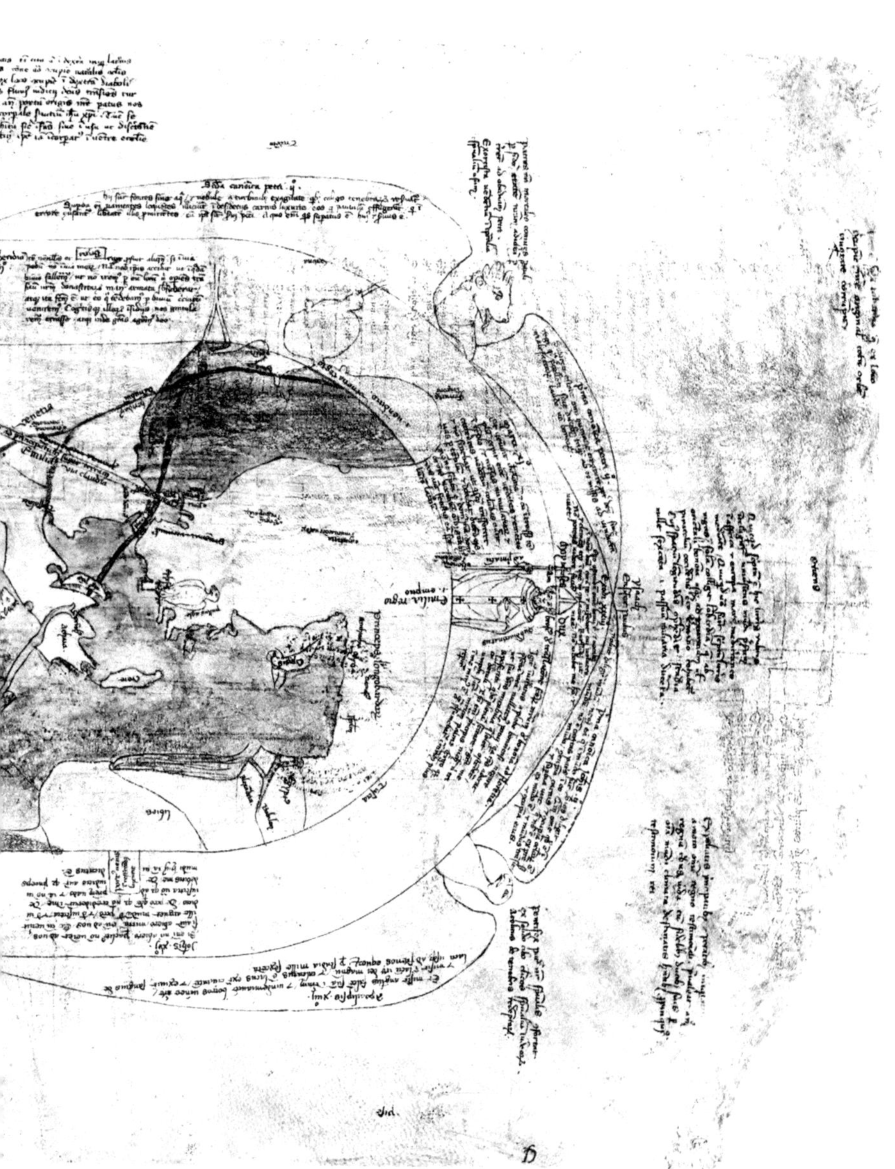

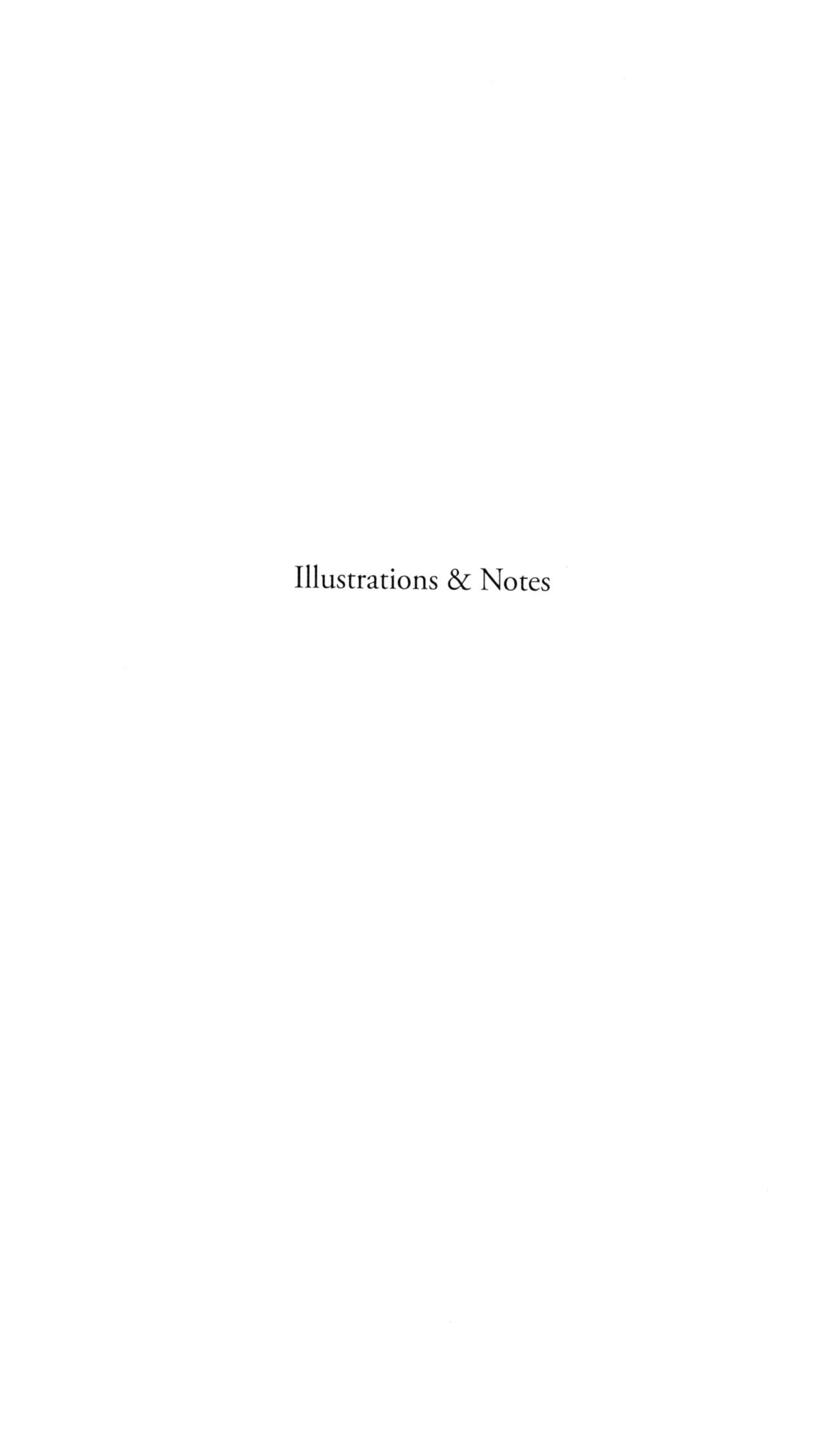

Illustrations & Notes

Cover Pen & ink drawing by the author, c. 2010, untitled.

I *Hawk*, painting by the author.

II French stamp "Coq d'Alger", 20 francs. Designed by Henry Razous, engraved by charles hervé, in cic-ulation between 15-11-1944 and 12-05-1945

III *Venus and Mars*, Veronese, 1570, Metropolitan Museum of Art, New York.

IV The photograph was taken during the battle of Pass-chendaele, 31 July to 6 November 1917, between the Allies and the German Empire. Passchendaele is in Belgium.

V Medieval illustrations have no known artist. They are open-sourced on the internet.

VI *Portrait of Prince Balthazar Charles in Hunting Dress*, Diego Velazquez, 1635, Museo del Prado, Madrid. Balthazar Charles was the child of King Phillip IV of Spain. In this 1635 portrait by Diego Velazquez, he is in his hunting costume and holds a child-sized shot gun. The name of his dog has been forgotten. Velazquez painted seven portraits of Balthazar Charles. The boy died of small pox in 1646 at age 16.

VII *Wheatfield with Crows*, Vincent Van Gogh, 1890, Van Gogh Museum, Amsterdam.

VIII *The Temptation of St Anthony* (detail), Hieronymus Bosch, 1501, Museu Nacional de Arte Antiqa, Lisbon.

IX *The Temptation of St Anthony* (detail), Hieronymus Bosch, 1501, Museu Nacional de Arte Antiqa, Lisbon.

X *The Temptation of St Anthony* (detail), Hieronymus Bosch, 1501, Museu Nacional de Arte Antiqa, Lisbon.

The Temptation of St Anthony, Hieronymus Bosch, 1501. Museu Nacional de Arte Antiqa, Lisbon. There exist numerous copies of *The Temptation of St Anthony*, but the version in Lisbon is considered to be the original.

XI *Martyrdom of Saint Pancratius*, stained glass window in in the Grote Kerk, Dordrecht, Netherlands.

XII Medieval miniature of a boar hunt. Hubert had vision of the cross suspended between the horns of the stag he chased and was instantly converted. Hubert became the patron saint of hunters, including the boar hunters this poem memorializes. St. Hubert is also a line of non-dairy fats, like margarine, all without palm oil.

XIII The mosaic depicting Odysseus tied to the mast and sneaking a look at the ladies while his crew looks in the other direction is Roman, 3rd century BCE. It is in the Bardo National Museum, Tunis. The Sirens were originally conceived of as half bird, half woman, suggesting to me that they were dream creatures, more like the succubus than ladies of the rue.

XIV Delphic Oracle on a wine cup, a kylix, Attic red on black, circa 440 BCE. The piece is in the Alte National Galerie, Berlin. Note her delicate feet.

XV Scene in Ypres, Belgium, after the battle of Pass-chendaele. The photograph was taken in 1918 and is in the public domain.

XVI Image from one of the Indian film director Satyajit Ray's movies. Ray wrote and directed a trilogy of films called the *Apu Trilogy* (1955-1959) which are considered among the most lyrical and beautiful movies ever made, true masterpieces. Ray was given an honorary Oscar by the Academy of Motion Pictures in 1992.

XVII The Hindu Goddess Parvati. Tamil Nadu, India, 11th century. Los Angeles County Museum of Art.

XVIII

The Priestess of Delphi, is by John Maler Collier (1850-1934). He is identified as a Pre-Raphaelite, a British movement of painters who specialized in sentimental eroticism and blush-toned semi-naked

XIX nymphs.

Antique Qing Dynasty (1636-1912) Chinese celadon glazed jar.

XX *Mont Sainte-Victoire with Large Pine*, Paul Cezanne, 1887, The Courtauld Gallery, London.

XXI *Hortense In a Red Dress*, Paul Cézanne, 1888. The Metropolitan Museum New York. M. Fiquet, the tour guide in this poem, *Saint-Victoire and Hortense*, is the grand nephew of Marie-Hortense Fiquet (1850-1922) who was the wife of Paul Cezanne and his frequent model. Cézanne painted 29 portraits of her, either because he loved her or because she was available and patient. How M. Fiquet ended up in Greece is unknown.

XXII World map by Opicinus de Canistris (1296-1353). He was an Italian priest, mystic, and cartographer of imaginary worlds.

Acknowledgements

This collection was enhanced by editorial advice and support from the poet Anne Harding Woodworth, the writers Jim Levy and Michele Zackheim, artists Elena Mudd, Charlie Ramsburg, and David Maes, who also designed the book, friends Isabelle Grasset, Mariana and Michael Kurko, Samuel Mudd, Maryse Tonnelier, Tom and Elise Noble, Pauline Fry, and above all my partner, Ellen Davies.